POETRY NOW

NORTHERN IRELAND

1993

Edited by Pat Wilson

First published in Great Britain in 1993 by
POETRY NOW
4 Hythegate, Werrington,
Peterborough, PE4 7ZP

All Rights Reserved

Copyright Contributors 1993

FOREWORD

Although we are a nation of poetry writers we are accused of not reading poetry and not buying poetry books: after many years of listening to the incessant gripes of poetry publishers, I can only assume that the books they publish, in general, are books that most people do not want to read.

Poetry should not be obscure, introverted, and as cryptic as a crossword puzzle: it is the poet's duty to reach out and embrace the world.

The world owes the poet nothing and we should not be expected to dig and delve into rambling discourse searching for some inner meaning.

The reason we write poetry (and almost all of us do) is because we want to communicate: an idea; or a specific feeling. Poetry is as essential in communication, as a letter; a radio; a telephone, and the main criteria for selecting the poems in this anthology is very simple: they communicate.

Faced with hundreds of poems and a limited amount of space the task of choosing the final poems is difficult and as editor one has to try to be as detached as possible - quite often editors can become a barrier in the writer-reader exchange - acting as go between, making the connection, not censoring because of personal taste.

In this volume around one hundred and sixty poems are presented to the reader for their enjoyment. The subject matter is as varied as the writers themselves, love, hate, war, peace, the seasons, etc.

The poetry is written on all levels; the simple and the complex both having their own appeal.

The success of this collection, and all previous Poetry Now anthologies, relies on the fact that there are as many individual readers as there are writers, and in the diversity of styles, subjects, and forms there really is something to please, excite, and hopefully, inspire everyone who reads the book.

This is a book that is a representative collection of poetry as it is being written today: POETRY NOW.

Contents

Title	Author	Page
Tory 1983 - 1992	Philip Cummings	1
An Evening in May	Andrew Collins	2
Where Can I Go?	Joan E Cunning	3
Re-birth	Pearl Reynolds	4
Michael	Patricia Newman	5
Two Men on a Raft	Francie McFaul	6
Charlotte's Kitten	Carol Slowey	7
Son of No Country	Robert White	8
I Can See	Declan O'Hara	9
Mo Ghrá Thú	Timothy Gillen	10
Ode to Pan	Gary Deans	11
Ireland	Mae McClean	12
Isolation	Gerard Martin	13
The Letter	Joseph Doyle	14
Through the Grate	Padraig Moore	15
War Poem	Eamon McAllister	16
In a Limavady Churchyard Nov 1991	Gerald Moorehead	17
The State of the Nation	N F McLoughlin	18
Ben - Victim of Aids	Colin Harris	19
Power of Love	Adele Norton	21
Doggerel	Philippa Robinson	22
Brave December Heart	R Barnett	23
No Change!	John Carr	24
Love	Robert Howard	25
A 20th Century Punk	John Deeham	27
Stagnant	Gerard McMonagle	28
As Everything Changes	Paul Donaghy	30
Stange Mind!	Gail Turner	31
Once in a Lifetime	Annie Lynch	32
Erin	Fred Baxter	33
Visit to the Graveyard after Sunday Mass	Sean Markey	34
Tyranny	Irene Duggleby	35
Let the Night Distil its Tears	Gearóid ó Gallchobhair	36

Night Catches Day	Eamonn Quinn	37
Slieve Donard (1989)	Andrew Casey	38
Views of a Mountain	Mark Trainort	39
Corner Boys	Alison J White	40
The Clown	John McCullagh	41
Dream of Damascus	Anne McLaughlin	42
Gollan Hill	Jack Porter	43
Wounded	Robin Brown	44
The Fire Burning Low	Giles McCay	45
On the Boa Island	Jane Wright	46
A Day in January	Conail Rutherford	47
No Man's Land	Rodney Archer	48
Brethren Bold	Samuel McCarter	49
Hear Me	Bernadette McLaughlin	50
The Old Place	Eileen Monaghan	51
Ordinary People	Eve Williams	52
Loss	John Maxwell	53
Where is my Homeland?	Margaret Campbell	55
Lovers	Damien McIntyre	56
A Cosmic Dream	Ernie Larkin	57
She's the One	Maurice Mahon	58
Few Thoughts	Louise Doherty	59
First Love	Patricia Todd	60
Beneath the Stone	Jeremy McLucas	61
A Memory	Lillian E Devlin	62
North Atlantic Nightmare	Paul Taggart	63
Préamhaca	Sorcha Nic An tSagairt	64
6th Form Study	Deirdre Devine	65
Jerusalem	Sean Lynch	66
The Waterfall	Claire Davidson	67
Untitled	Rhona Andrews	68
Garden	Paul McClafferty	69
If No-One Comes	Maura Johnston	70
On the Bus	Aideen Devine	71
Twilight	Gerard Craig	72
Last Rites	Stephen McCauley	73
Born Again Heroes	John Harkin	74

Metamorphosis	Gladys Mulligan	76
The Amethyst Hills	Rosaleen Clarke	77
Vows	Una Walsh	78
Baking	Ann Keith-Sandford	79
A Loved One So Dear	Anita Jackson	80
The Voyage of Brendan	Lawrence Price	81
The Dangerous Hobbies of Johnny Blackbeard MP	Thomas I Maguire	82
The Mouse	James Coyle	83
Silences	Nicholas Laird	84
Circle	Liam Porter	85
Grey Point in June	Kathleen Baillie	86
Derry	Mary Josephine Devlin	87
Earth Matters	L V Wilson	88
A Sonnet to Mozart	J A Sinton	89
Easter Roulette	Win Harwood	90
Orogeny	Séan Greer	91
Solitude	A M Chambers	92
And then the Frost	Maureen Smyth	93
The Little I Keep	Daniel Spencer Harley	94
Alpha and Omega	Joan Crossan	95
Time	Michael Beare	96
Story to a Young Daughter	G Wills	97
War and Peace	Ethna Johnston	98
False Justice	James Jackson	99
Perfect Union	Sean McWilliams	100
Self Destruction	Mary Carson	101
Childhood Friend	Jacqueline McGregor	102
Dispossession	Sharon McCleery	103
Artemis Dream Forgotten	Raymond Dinsmore	104
Here	Kevin Meehan	105
A Quiet Place	Gary Allen	106
Impressions	Joseph Allen	107
A Season's Touch	Theresa Rafferty	108
For Yorick: Late August	J C Nelson	109
Magic	John Corvan	110
November Admiral	John McCabe	111

Title	Author	Page
A Winter Zoo	Arthur Campbell	112
Untitled	T P McNamee	113
Belfast Telegraph	Joseph Boucher	114
The Word	Desmond Durkan	115
Growing Old with the Day	Liam Quigley	116
Sacrifice	Niall Grimes	117
Old House in Tamlaghtmore	Thomas Spiers	118
The Craft of the Hermaphrodite	Simon D Leeman	119
The Glories of War	David Rogers	120
Peanuts - Crisp, Dry Yet Salty	Paul Kelly	121
Himself	Lil Brady	122
To Break a Butterfly	Rhoda Quinn	123
A View From the Sky	Nicola Doherty	124
Untitled	R Griffin	125
My Mournes	Emily Bronte Taylor	126
The Literary Maiden's Lament or Men I Just Couldn't Marry and One I could	Myra Dryden	127
Madame Butterfly on the Terrace	Claire Marie Norris	129
Fond Memories	Trina Porter	130
Synthetic Reality	Ken Grimason	131
Up Spake the Champion	Ken Adams	132
Which Way?	Cora Cassidy	133
A Love Poem	Muriel Cameron	134
Essence	Marleen Rajan	135
Pecking Order	Bernie McClelland	136
Emotions	Kathleen Canville	137
Loneliness	Gráinne McCay	138
Arrival at the Factory	Gilbert N Thorpe	139
Woman vs Woman	Geraldine McIlmurray	140
Cherry Blossom	Anne Cairns	141
Northern Ireland (1993)	Norah Brown	142
Night Shifts	Jim Davidson	143
On Buying a Poinsettia	Sandra Elwood	144
Life	Richard Wilson	145

The Preacher Man	Maggie Mayberry	146
Faded	Michael Hegarty	147
By the Seaside	John McGowan	148
Moonrise	Richard Ross	149
Untitled	Richard McLaughlin	150
Untitled	Ian McLaughlin	151
Childhood Fragments	Lisè Watson	152
Alone	Frankie Quinn	153
Lourdes	Frances Doyle	154
First Five Days	Peter Hough	155
The Cost of Being Loyal	Mary Quigley	156
Kangaroo Court	Liam O'Comáin	157
The Singing Soldier	Paul Hutton	158
Promenade	Paul Laughlin	159
The Nightmare	R G Harkness	160
The Mirage Fades as the Cold Appears	Terence S McGivern	161
Realisations	Seamus Sarsfield	162
Spider Spell	Liam Black	163
Dawn's Early Light	Norman Newell	164

Tory 1983 - 1992

Sitting by the Tau Cross wondering
When you asked me for a dance,
Four years ago last August,
The church-hall half empty
And the bare boards echoed my refusal;
Had you more than dancing on your mind?

I left five minutes later
And found this sacred site,
Watched the house lights twinkling on the mainland
Through the softness of the night.
I ached to hear the fall of footsteps
Coming down the hill,
But you didn't answer my proposal,
And now you never will.

Philip Cummings

An Evening in May

An evening in May,
I find my love,
Sitting on a bundle of hay,
Her summer complexion,
And strawberry hair,
Melts the mood that stirs in my heart.
From the broken style,
In the middle of the field,
I go down on bended knee,
And propose to her.
My cheeks flush with anticipation,
As the words,
'I do'
Trickle from her delicious mouth.
My heart bursts into song,
As the evening fills with love
And happiness.
I shall never forget,
This evening in May.

Andrew Collins

Where Can I Go?

Where can I go -
When friendship has lost its glow?
To whom can I run -
When the long, lonely day is done?
My tiny ship has been tossed and battered
Upon the stormy sea,
Who can I call upon
If I cannot turn to thee?

I am ready to set sail again,
I fear not the surge of the raging tide,
You will come to my rescue -
When others cast me aside,
You are willing to love me,
Your soft voice is gentle and kind,
Taking my hand in yours,
When the rest all leave me behind.

What can I do Lord?
I can kneel and pray,
You are my true friend, my consolation,
You abide with me, night and day,
Your presence will strengthen and
       guide me,
Your love will never cease,
Leading me onward -
To a lasting haven of peace.

Joan E Cunning

Re-birth

The gentle breeze brushes the hillside,
And the sun, golden in its splendour
Sends too its kiss of pardon
On the girl,
Crushed by sin and shame,
Who kneels now
At Jesus' feet.
Never had man spoken to her
Like this Man
Whose kind eyes hold
The mysteries of Eternity
And before whom
Evil holds no power.
Lovingly He raises her up,
Cleansed and forgiven,
And in the peace of this hillside
Mary Magdalene is re-born.

Pearl Reynolds

Michael

'You shouldn't have done that.
You shouldn't have done that.'
A Derry woman's voice screams
in anger, then in grief
Cutting through the grey Saturday air.
She cradles his hurt head in her lap
and whispers,
'Hush now love, you'll be alright,'
As his life's blood flows down a wet
Shipquay street
Under the feet of stunned shoppers.
He is now paying the ultimate price
for wearing the dark-green uniform.
How could his blinkered assassin know
Michael was a Catholic.

(In memory of Michael Ferguson, a young
policeman killed last Saturday 23-1-92 in Derry
and all who have suffered in our confusion.

Patricia Newman

Two Men on a Raft

I saw two men on a raft.
One says he's Irish,
The other one British.
Both have to survive.
So how do they do it!
With their similar history, from opposite sides,
A common language with uncommon ties,
And a form of religion with strange little twists.
So both of them curse and put up their fists,
And I saw two men on a raft..........

Francie McFaul

Charlotte's Kitten

Wanting a kitten so hard
The want gnawed at her heart
'Til she sought for herself
An almost comfort
In the small soft weight of
A stone covered with fur.

Carol Slowey

Son of No Country

Son of no country
Child of no God
The rivers dry, my seasons star
Is rust within the thorny soil.

Land of my anger
Church of my pain
In midnight streets where old ghosts dance
Their poison to the breaking day.

Lies of my fathers
Sins of my sons
The famine breath and marching eyes
Shall stumble trapped in His strangling love.

Son of no country
Child of no god
The river swells, a seasons prayer
Is dust upon a border road.

Robert White

I Can See

Black, awakes me.
Light chrome
Yellow
Mid chrome, adjust my eyes.
Light orange
Orange
Light red, warm me.
Red
Deep red
Scarlet, prepare the morning.
Mid blue
Bright green
Deep green, colour-match my day.
Deep blue
Navy blue, tire me.
Brown
Black, make me sleep.

Declan O'Hara

Mo Ghrá Thú
   (I love you)

If this is love
I don't want to be here anymore
Locked in this dark room
That numbs my brain
And freezes the life in my soul.
Take me from this place,
Let me go back to the warm places of my mind
Where I can soar free
And touch a happiness that I have not yet known.
Have I known love?
Or have I known a fear,
A fear of the truth?
Have I hid behind some romantic notion
And lost myself in foolishness?
I want to walk in a meadow of white flowers
Under our favourite star
And talk of poetry and songs,
I want to hear the healing of your voice
And touch a love I know is true.
Have I found you?
Or am I hoping in vain
Again?

Timothy Gillen

Ode to Pan

Earth bone, standing stone,
The piper calls the tune.
Forest Lord with room to roam,
To chase and catch the moon,
Emerald, wood flesh throne,
Wild spirit of the tree,
His being is believing,
His essence mystery.
Water blood, river foam,
magic, mystique, night,
Dream that bright reality,
Hear the wind-wood pipes.
Soil skin, kith and kin,
Whispers in the wind,
Apple blossom scent the air,
Bracken, hawthorn, whin,
Stand upon the gates of dawn,
From hoof, through heart to horn,
Primal, sacred, wordless song,
That's green womb born.

Gary Deans

Ireland

When you think of Ireland what does it conjure up for you?
A picture of a mountain shrouded in morning dew?
Or do you think of a valley with hills on either hand?
Or a quite tranquil beach with miles of golden sand?

It is a land of contrasts, on this we will agree
With its woodlands, lakes and rivers, bounded by the sea
The grass it is the greenest that you have ever seen
Even the rain is gentle and the sunshine is a dream!

A land rich in folklore, stories told of old
Of rainbows and leprechauns, and pots full of gold
Of gnomes, elves and fairies - and even trees that moan
Could you imagine Ireland without the Blarney Stone?

A land of much culture, of music and of art
Where dancing and drama all play a part
The people here are friendly, they make you feel carefree
And they've always been reputed for their hospitality.

It is my native country, the land I love so well
I'll always sing it's praises and of it's beauty tell
There are other islands with treasures rich and rare
But there is not another that can with it compare.

So you think I'm 'selling' Ireland, well that's not strictly true
We like you all to visit us, there's a welcome here for you,
'Not selling' I say and you ask the reason why,
Some things are really priceless, which even money cannot buy.

Mae McClean

Isolation

A knock at the door
And I go to the window
To look out
There stands a stranger
Collar up and face turned away
I do not know this man.

What could he want?
He knocks again
And yet I do not go
I cannot, just in case
The news is bad.

Another knock much louder than before
And yet I stand quite still
I watch him leave and disappear
This stranger at my door.

Gerard Martin

The Letter

We have not spoken for so long
It seems to me so very wrong
That you want me to speak first
That I simply can not do.

I know you're on your own
Just pick up the telephone
And say you love me
As I love you.

It is easy as you can see
Please do not leave me in Coventry
If you speak first
It will end all this strife.

I am waiting for your call
Then there will be no wall
And we will get together
To start a new life.

Joseph Doyle

Through the Grate

Red hot embers,
Shadowed by overhanging logs,
Like the sun rising over the
Mountain in a wild western scene.

And the draft sweeping down the chimney,
For a moment totally extinguishing the bright
Glowing coals,
Like the sun occasionally being lost behind the clouds.

Suddenly,
From out of a ravine,
Sprung a flame.
Browning the bark of an Alder tree,
And tinting the turf above.

Far off volcanoes erupt,
As short puffs of smoke bellow from between coals.
Occasionally followed by a small flickering flame
In the midst of the smoke.

Flames resting on logs,
Like the tide washing up onto the golden beach,
While others dance upon the coals in silence.

Padraig Moore

War Poem

'Rise lads! signalled the sergeant,
        a new day has begun.
A day of continuous fighting,
        endless fighting,
Guns blazing, bodies dropping aimlessly,
Explosions and bullets making patterns,
        in the air above me. . .

I watch the sky become
        darker and darker
                through the day
                      and saw,
How much nature was being destroyed,
        not one tree to be seen,
Not one leaf of grass to grow. . .

        At my side,
I saw two solders slump to the ground,
Two bullet wounds marked their heads.
        that will be more bodies for
        burial the next day. . .

        The day at last, darkens,
Lighted again by explosions in the sky,
        a new day begins.
'Rise lads!' signalled the sergeant.

Eamon McAllister

In a Limavady Churchyard Nov 1991

Twenty-four names, ranks and numbers,
The long, the short and the tall,
Lined up in regimental fashion,
In response to the clarion call.
Young lions urged by bungling donkeys,
Prepared such innocents to fall,
Lined up in regimental fashion,
To be slaughtered one and all.
Standard issue serried headstones,
Ever static to 'Close Order' bawl,
Lined up in regimental fashion,
Along this rimy graveyard wall.

'Smile boys, thats the style'.

Gerald Moorehead

The State of the Nation

Rhetoric, religion, bullets and bricks,
Pandora had no such box of tricks;
Yet Pandora's box did hope contain,
In this land no hope - just pain.

Who will sever this Gordian knot?
Did human hand pen this thickening plot?
Conspiring Fates create in scholars hell,
To torture saints with a land's death knell.

Here Democles' sword hangs over all,
By slender thread - and it must fall;
Where will it fall? When? On whom?
How many bodies will fill this tomb?

All are judged both foes and friends,
The balance sways - one side descends;
The sins of the father are now passed down,
In this maelstrom all are drowned.

N F McLoughlin

Ben - Victim of Aids

Go towards the light, just leave behind the pain
Enough suffering, enough tears, time to let go
No more tubes or wires clinging to this beautiful child
An angel of light and courage, in Heaven undefiled.

'Will you put my bike in the paper Mom,
- I don't think I need it anymore'
A spirit being gently beckoned, guided to the light
His little frame is bolstered somehow with a majesty and might.

'Can I go round to Jessica's Mom,
I really miss her, she's my best friend'
But Jessica's gone now, gone toward the light
Mom's had to tell him, Jessica died last night.

'Do you like Megatron too!
He's my favourite cartoon of all'
Just lie in bed now, watch T.V. or talk
The little guy's too sick, even to take a walk.

'Will I go to Heaven?
Mom, Dad, tell me about it!'
And its just like a holiday, when you come home
A haven of love, where you'll never be alone.

'But Mom, will I know anyone there?
Is Jessica in Heaven Mom?'
Grandpa is there, Grandma is there, Jessica is there too
They're waiting little Ben when its time for you.

The time has come, the very moment is here
Ben's walking down the tunnel, the light is getting near
'Goodbye Mom, Goodbye Dad, I love you
- and world, will you love me too?

Colin Harris

Power of Love

The quality of my love is outstanding
To perfection and grace it will infix
No one has found a love so great
How lucky my love on your path I was put.
Break open your heart upon me
My thirst is so strong like a gale
Pour out your blood let me taste
Let your body and soul near my touch.
Don't be retracted from my power
I'm like a breeze in the night
Through every key hole I'll reach to you.
I'll cherish your arms stretched before me
I can't reverse given feelings
My hearts law won't permit
You are it's reason to expand out for more love
Don't go away, our love in life is a fulfilment.

Adele Norton

Doggerel

By bands of asphalt our space is riven
So that vehicles can be driven
Resource - exhausting, the bus, van and car -
With noise and stench the landscape they mar.
Pedestrians' spirit and freedom are 'kerbed'
But no-one will speak a dissenting word
As we meekly wait for the traffic to part -
For we are co-opted, soul and heart
As country lanes are widened to roads
With motor travel our universe explodes -
To reach the city centre for fifty pence,
We abandon local shops and natural sense.

The human race abides and stays mum,
But look at the animals we call 'dumb'
The band of canines are at least astute
Enough to detest the vehicle route.
Assembled they wait in angry pose -
Scenting which way the carbon monoxide blows,
Then run and bark and snap their jaws,
Risking life and limb to fight for a lost cause.

Philippa Robinson

Brave December Heart

There she is, that pal at the pool-side,
Laughing, plunging, swimming.
So strong and full of life.
Blond, freckled, with a tall, athletic frame.

There she is, nurse at the R.V.H.,
Doctor's spouse, mother of three, pianist, artist,
Home-nurse, golfer, traveller,
Cook, party-giver, friend;
Patient, jet-setter, property-owner,
Grandmother two times over, wife of Coral years,
Reader, swimmer...

There she was,
Suddenly,
At rest!
She who was so seldom still.
Found by her second-born son
On a black December day,
(under the sunny skies of Tenerife).

And now, we face a bleak New Year,
Sad and empty without her...
Yet thankful and hopeful too;
Deeply touched and freshly warmed
By that lass at the pool-side,
Brave, smiling, friend of our youth.

R Barnett

No Change!

Tramps apathetically walk under ladders, sleep in subways
And hug kerbs and corners.
Some have their sores licked by a passing mutt,
Others fight over a quality cardboard box.

They are not concerned with mortgage repayments,
Interest rates, nor currency values.
Some too stupid to commit a crime, long for the
Relative comfort of a prison cell.

A mother and child, huddling outside a bank no less.
Lifeless like the mannequins in the shop windows,
Weathered like the pavement beneath them.
Holding out a lunchbox, as empty as themselves.

They see, only shoes, of all colours, types and sizes.
Exhaust fumes choke their cries for a mere coin or two.
Their energy drained as they sit beside a gutter,
Sadly bringing a new dimension to the word 'affiliation'.

A blind woman perched outside an opticians,
Keeping track of the time as the town clock chimes.
Rush hour represents her best hour,
As people stop, stare and show they care.

She relies on her remaining senses.
The blaring of car horns and the chill of the north wind,
The trail of fast food and the piles in her posterior.
If only others had the same sense of awareness.

A muttering of 'any change?' is heard,
Yet people cross to the other side of the street.
Those that don't answer, 'no change!',
Opening their mouths before their brains are engaged.
John Carr

Love

With every turning of every tide,
The shoreline has no escape, or haven to hide,
From the sea, stealing the sand.
In all its glory and all its pride,
It advances and retreats in one relentless stride.
The sand is a puppet, only being controlled at will.
Two lovers, they are parted only to return,
In a whirlwind of passion and love.
The time they have together is short,
But life for me holds but a fraction in comparison.
What I can create and give to others may bring a smile,
Or lighten a heart.
But the ultimate manufacturer of magnificence holds all to
Control,
And has bequeathed onto me a heart.
A gift of life,
A gift for my pleasure.
Now I find myself like a shoreline, and my heart has been
Disrupted,
Tampered with,
And wisdom, and sense, and calm, have deserted me and I have
Found something new.
The power of my discovery overpowers even the most brutal.
My conquering no saga.
Another gift, another thief.
I am dazed, feel sedated, feel anger
Oh tremendous anger, and why?
To describe my thief would be to insult Cleopatra.

With all of these gifts I have been granted,
I dare ask more, grant her the understanding,
Grant her the power.
She ridicules me.
I cower at her feet.
I am blinded by what I see.
Will ever she retreat from my shoreline?

Robert Howard

A 20th Century Punk

Call me crazy, call me wild
But don't call me stupid or I'll do you
For I know, you know who does this
Who takes away our brains
We even know the reason
It's their revenge.

They were young once
Now they're old, dying out
And they tell the world we're dangerous
But that's so no-one will trust us
No-one will give a damn
It's their revenge.

But now we're getting stronger
Some day we'll rule the world
And bury all those fools who kept us down
Then is we feel the passion
To blow us all to hell
It's our revenge.

John Deeham

Stagnant

Clutter, clang, is bellowing through the monotonous
drone of civilisation.
The atmosphere in the house is unusually quiet, yet deafening
what is wrong?
My mother's face is torn between fear and anger.

I grabble up the mountain of stairs engulfing me in their immensity.
I clutch and crawl my way to the top.
I trail the old tool-box dripping with colours of Autumn,
and bring it to the window so I can stand on it and look out of my crows
nest.

The windows are clogged with smog by the demons of the night
a street lamplight glistens and glares in the dark musky night.
Condensation trickles and scarpers down the window gathering speed.
A spider's webb is dancing in the moonlight being coaxed by the gentle
night breeze.

I brush the window clear and the clutter and clanging is growing louder
and louder.
In the distance bizarre shapes of flame fly through the air
like dragon flies on a humid July night.

Streets are spewing out with crowds, the flames continue to fly through the
air
And on impound explode, how beautiful they thrust through the air, yet
on impact cause such destruction.

My mother's mouth is tensed her cheeks taut,
gazing in desperation as blood and sweat burned so sickeningly easily.
As I begin to comprehend what has happened I cry,
but feeling unforgiving hatred and disgust.

I stood there fists clenched, veins bubbling, vowing to myself it will be different when I grow up.
But now I don't need that tool-box to look out of my crows nest, yet it still goes on and on and on.

Gerard McMonagle

As Everything Changes

Autumn turns to winter
As winter turns to spring
Spring becomes the summer and
Summer is everything
Daytime turns to night-time
Night-time becomes the day
As everything changes
The more things stay the same.

Nations turn to empires
As empires turn to dust
Dust becomes a light veneer on
Treasures full of rust
Daytime turns to night-time
Night-time becomes the day
As everything changes
The more things stay the same.

Girl becomes a woman
As boy becomes a man
Cupid shoots his arrow out
Across their broken land
Love will last forever
Love will never decay
As everything changes
The more things stay the same.

Paul Donaghy

Strange Mind!

The fulfilment repels the desire.
Why desire an outcome and then
Reject the awaited response?
What provokes the refusal and
Reticence?
What barrier surfaces like the back
Of a swimming dolphin
- invisible and then clearly visible
Diving through the water?

Strange mind! Who can fathom you?
What are your reasons?
Tautness in the heart - why do you
Appear and force me to feel you?
Dipping unseeing into the depths,
Scrabbling around for a definitive
Concept.
Almost caught - but elusively
Fragmenting,
Broken by the ripples caused trying
To reach you.
Be still - it may yet surface and
Silently pause - clearly definable
And unaware that it is being watched.

Gail Turner

Once in a Lifetime

On the morning of the 17th August 89',
The earth and moon came into line.
A total eclipse of the moon took place
Very few people saw it, what a disgrace.
A once in a lifetime sight was beheld,
When silver, darkened turned to red.
Earth passed on, on it's eternal flight,
As a new day dawned from darkened
Night.

Annie Lynch

Erin

O Erin thou are torn with pain
And strife that should not be
I fain would share thy sadness
For thou art dear to me.

How can it be that men should strive
With fevered brow and hearts that burn
To win thee that can ne'er be won
Who lovest all and favourest none?

Why is it so that men should die
And women weep and children cry
Amidst thy beauty, land and sea
Bestowed on all so graciously?

God grant thee peace and calm and rest
That quiet be thy troubled breast
When swords to ploughshares men shall beat
And sit as brothers round thy feet.

Then thou who knew us in the womb
And shall embrace within the tomb
Shall joy as all the world shall see
Thee blest with saint and scholarly.

Fred Baxter

Visit to the Graveyard after Sunday Mass

The squeak of the gate.
An octave of difference
From the raucous crows.

Red-coated women with cream shoes
Grey hatted grey men.
Sunday's best!

Standstills reflective
Respectful respective.
With whispered prayers and pleas
Blown aloft to join
The whispers of the dancing leaves.

Icy droplets on the ends of red noses
Everything in this place cold.
A comfortable hot dinner to go home to
Quick!

Sleepers arranged
Neatly in rows.
Know your place
Dormatorium ultimum.

Lights Out!

Sean Markey

Tyranny

How can they sleep at night
these fiends that plot to kill?
Who kid themselves they've made it 'right'
Phoning to admit their skill.

Children, women, men of all ages,
Interests are to maim.
Enacting their 'Deed' at various stages
By planting bombs - what do they gain?

Knowing they have caused destruction
Do these cowards receive a thrill?
To blast and demolish without compunction
Hopefully, the decay and rot *Inside* will kill.

Irene Duggleby

Let the Night Distil its Tears

Let the night distil it's tears
In an outrage of darkness
And slippery stars in frost
Beneath the lord protector's drunken hoof
And glisten and shine on the courthouse roof
To lull his children back to sleep,
Back to their pot-holed dreams
On border roads
That rise above the sentinel snores
And lidless eyes in the whin bush
That gauge the marrow in the bone
The thought in the head
The strut in the step
The walker at night
And name and address of the dark
And shout aloud in the searching fear
Despite the barbed wire dreams: 'We are here'
Let the night time sleep it's fill
In barbed wire beds
And justice rest it's head
In a maze of sandbag pillows.
Foreign voices at the drystone walls
Are lisping questions at the willow trees
And catalogue the leaves in files
So that all the sleepers rest assured
That every tree is certified and cured
And in them evil does not grow
But voices shout aloud in the searching fear
And name and address of the wind
The age of the sky, occupation of trees
Despite the barbed wire dreams, 'We are here'.

Gearóid ó Gallchobhair

Night Catches Day

Night springs unexpected unto day
It's raining tears
Bursting forth like ugly flowers
Into blossoms.
Lightning licks the sky,
The waters swirl, swish and shwoo for cover.

I put the book away
Gazing out
Waiting or something,
Nothing comes,
Except the sound of a radio below,
A lonesome sax solo
Staccato notes pebble-dashing the wall of the storm.

50s blues blending with 90s torment
Unholy and unstoppable night
Time and space skipping light
Dancing across the Earth,
As I crawl under dreamless sheets,
Waiting for sleep
Like a lover to come.

Eamonn Quinn

Slieve Donard (1989)

I stand by the mound of stones beside the triangulation station
On Ulster's highest mountain on a shiny, bright day.
The Mournes below plunge into the Irish Sea.
I linger, lazing, by the sheltering stones.

Soon I must return to reality, to depravity,
To Newcastle, the old railway and shimmering sea.
A last glance at England, murmuring miles away,
And the coast as far as the Ards.
Is this wild and desolate beauty unmatched?

Clumsily tumbling through bogs, rocks and heather
To the track, which is a stormy stream in Winter,
Trudging through trees to the foot of the mountain.

Exhausted, elated, I eat and sleep.
A lovely day has passed so quickly.
I see the mound from where I stand,
Admiring the splendour of this land.

Andrew Casey

Views of a Mountain

Night...
On a windy beach at Cushendall I first
Saw your image silhouetted against a purple
Blue night sky.
The full bright moon shone silver across the bay
Throwing white waves onto the shore.
Standing among the Glens knowing your own
Security, how I long to be like you.

Misty day...
I once walked your gentle summit surrounded
By a creeping mist that consumed the fields
And valleys around.
All about that white wall of uncertain distance
Kept me from viewing the scenes below that I love.
Everywhere the presence of ancient warriors
Hang in the air.
Brave men who used your high vantage point
Defending their time, they left scars
For all to see.

Whenever...
You mean so much to me I can hardly say
Appropriate words standing in your gaze.
Knowledge seeps from you
And spills down on rainy days as tears of a mountain
For so many years you've stood and guarded
This beautiful corner of my world, a debt
I can never hope to repay.

Mark Trainort

Corner Boys

'Get out'
'Get out from under my feet'.

No job to go to
No deadline to meet.
Pubs not yet open -
No place to go
To talk through the night's watching,
The long day of woe.
So we meet on the corner
And lean on the wall
To watch the sun rising
And feel the rain fall.
'No hope' is our motto
As time will not heal
The rift of employment
The loss that we feel.
We drift through each day
And pass on the time
Always waiting and watching
The cars on the Line.
With each day we grow older,
And clothes show less care,
The young ones grow bolder
But we never care.

Yet deep in our hearts
We feel it's not right
To stand on the corner
All day 'til the night.

Alison J White

The Clown

Sometime after ten
The flaps were pulled aside on the circus tent
In Tommy Mooney's upper field
And wide-eyed children faced the darkness
Gripping tight to parents' hands and treading
On the slatted boards across the mud
To find the car and home to bed.
And all the way back they talked at fever pitch
About the clown
And tried to catch his shriek of joy
Or the shoulder rolling of his tousled head.
All next day at school
Their ambition stopped at the red nosed fool
Who let their spirits soar above
The gathering days of winter darkness.
In Madge's post office, which housed the only parish phone.
I saw the clown, defrocked that very day
Trying number after number on the black wall phone
With its starting handle to alert the exchange in Omagh.
She would tell me later that he was searching for his wife
Who ran away the day before
With the serious little man who sat in the caravan near Mooney'g gate
Collecting the tickets to see the circus
And the clown.

John McCullagh

Dream of Damascus

Darkness to light
The essential flight
Needs digging
Dumping delving
In strange lands
Sand lands.

Even deserts
In their way
Speak and move
To contentment
Under stars
And midnight sky.

Not you, not I
Restlessness lies
In crouched pose
Spear the speech
That will search
The wild wonders
Of skies and peaks.

Freshen to glistening hue
Diffuse the unspeakable
Fresh found truth
To the glory of One
Who missions all
To seek to be.

Anne McLaughlin

Gollan Hill

Gollan benignly gazes down on somnolent Buncrana Town,
High on her gorse-emblazoned braes, knee-deep in fern, the oxen stray.
Browsing on heather-fragrant lawn, on pasture dew-tipped ere the dawn.

She slumbers in the morning sun, lulled by melodic murmurous hum,
Of droning bees pulsating love, of fragrant thyme and tall foxglove
By cuckoos' note wooing the morn, by landrails echo from the corn.

Serene she towers above White Strand, a crescent league of silvery sand,
She sees the shimmering swilly's sheen, alluring as an artists dream,
From Fanad light to Fair Inch Isle, a crystal lake reflects her smile
She sees each little boat that may emerge from Fahan, or Salon Bay
The sea-birds wheeling in its wake, weave willowy patterns in the lake.

She thrills as evening's freshening breeze so faintly stirs the leafy freeze,
Resplendent on Rathmullens shore, their evensong as oft before
Is thrilled by softly chiming bell, whose mellow tone she loves so well.

She sighs as shadows look askance,
At quivering waters sparkling dance
When murmurous waves begin to beat
In langourous rapture at her feet.
And low behind 'Knockallas' height
the glorious sun-set fades from sight.

Jack Porter

Wounded

Wounded, you would often cry -
- will it mend or leave a mark?
So tell me child of silken wood -
Will I mend?
Will I mark?

Robin Brown

The Fire Burning Low

Where the bird flies,
Where the wind blows,
Voices call him back.
Deep inside a memory
Of days gone by,
And a hope of
Days yet to come.
Days faded into night,
Faded into time;
And time left you behind:
A walking museum.
But the walls are crumbling down
With your relics, presence and sight.

Then, you too, will be remembered,
At least by me.
So, when you are dead
And your simple era gone, one will still remember,
Remember you. Your cap, stick,
Your house with hard floors,
And a stove to keep you alive.
But the fire is dying
And will soon be but a memory.

Giles McCay

On the Boa Island

Slab grey and cold, the shrouded waters shift
As, moving almost imperceptibly,
They edge towards the distant, western sea.
And from beneath the hanging clouds there drifts
An air of sorrow, like a leaden pall.
Even the smudged, green islands seem to mourn.
Their gnarled old oaks and twisted, choking thorns
Are burnt in umber, tainted through with gall.
Along the bouldered shore and on the reeds
The early morning glistens, tear-drop wet.
Is it the Celtic past that will not let
This listening place forget its widow's weeds?
For, in the sloe-dark grove at Boa,
Once Druids held their murky, ancient rites,
Made human sacrifices in the night
And worshipped runes about the mistletoe.
And now the Janus figure, as it looks both ways,
Recalls the dancing shadows and the screams
And holds the memory, as in a dream,
Locked deep within an androgynous gaze.

Jane Wright

A Day in January

It promised to come
And alas it has
A thin, temporary canopy
Of nervous ice
Sitting delicately on the cold
Dripping lush grass
Happy in the shadows
Shielded from the sun
As a fragile virgin.

Leaves and soaking twigs
Frozen in decay
Sparsely decorate this
Wedding cake
The most natural and free
To lie carpet of all
Slowly broken, consumed and
Forgotten

In melting tears the canopy collapses
Fragile promises of beauty
Eternity and glittering prizes
Drown in its echo
It promised to go
And alas it has.

Conail Rutherford

No Man's Land

Frozen fields lie silent in the full moonlight
Cold November feeling chills the bones,
Lifeless eyes reflect relentless darkness all around
As shivers charge the spine then turn to stone.

A God-forsaken landscape shames the old country,
Grotesque stands a gatepost like a mock head-stone,
Shocking breathless features, crooked broken limbs
Lie to be discovered, but for now disowned.

A shallow icy ditch in this no-man's land is
An obscene terminus that cries absurd.
The force of strong opinion buries many likewise here
A strange new testament for a strange new world.

A thaw will not commute this harsh reality,
The rigours of the season wild will return.
But stillness will envelope and stars bear witness,
Sure in that distant heart a flame still burns.

Rodney Archer

Brethren Bold

July skies shows
Signs of emotion.

Sheep run in
Groups, undecided
Which direction to
Turn.

A distant wind
Rolls the sound
Of a drum.

I restless sleepless
Toss and turn.

Samuel McCarter

Hear Me

The day never ends, and the night never falls,
I alternate from hazy light to shadowy gloom between
      these confining walls.
Laughter and music lie beyond my door. I can hear,
Though I'm not supposed to, do not disturb me, be
      solemn when you are near.
Slowly and piously come forward, to look and check,
See if I'm still breathing, and are the blankets
      pulled up to my neck.
Dust the statues silently, place them gently on the lace,
Sprinkle me with the Holy water, wouldn't do if I
      slipped out of grace.
Polish the drawers they've held my secrets for so many years,
Now they're at anyones disposal, all my memories, hopes
      and fears.
The smile, which used to greet my friends every day,
Is suspended now, sardonic in a glass, it seems to say,
'You'll not be needing me anymore, you who used to walk
      so erect and smart.
You're shoes, coats and umbrella became redundant, all
      you have left is the beat of your heart.'
But, I know that is not right,
      though I admit I must look a sight,
            as my body melts into my bed the
                  only bulges are my feet and head -
And my brain functions, its *my* witness that I'm not dead.

Bernadette McLaughlin

The Old Place

The peal of cathedral bells in the night
The trilling of birds as soon as it's light
The laughter of children running to school
The surge of the river refreshing and cool.

A ship's siren blowing down at the docks
The timely striking of our own Guildhall clock
An ambulance wails its impatient tattoo
As traffic pulls over to let it rush through.

These are the sounds of the Derry I know
I hear them in dreams, and I'm yearning to go
Back to my roots where a ghost will be lain
If I ever return to the old place again.

Eileen Monaghan

Ordinary People

In the beautiful land where I belong,
People live with many fears,
Where the ordinary people live their lives,
And cry their frustrated tears.

For here the never thinking few,
Force their own opinions by,
Attacking those with different beliefs,
And those around them are left to cry.

This violent minority,
Who will listen, will not cease,
Do not represent the people's views,
The wearied people long for peace.

Alone in bed I too have cried,
Weary and pitiful tears,
I can only pray for the end,
Of the trouble which exceeds my years.

Eve Williams

Loss
(For Paul who was killed, aged 15, by a bomb.)

His death came,
Like a door,
Slammed,
Like a kick on the head.

I cried,
The sight of his body,
The little pock marks
On his face.

His still warm back,
Negated his going,
So I asked again,
Is he dead?

Now I grieve,
Not for me,
But for
A perished potential.

He will not know physical fusion
Ever.
The coalescence of love.

He will not know
Procreation
Ever.
The joy-stick of birth.

He will not know
Others
Ever
The altruistic possibility.

He was born
Tabula RASA.
The slate,
Was not half filled.

John Maxwell

Where is my Homeland?

Where is my homeland - it is not here
'Tis a place where I shall eventually arrive at
As I journey, experiencing joy that sorrow
Snatches from me all too soon
Finding truths to dispel my doubts
Living with a mixture of mystery and wonderment
Feeling hopes rise and fall like the beat of a heart
Seeing dreams crumble
Beginning again - ready for another experience
Searching, learning, discovering the footprints of others
Who stumbled and fell as they too, made their way home
They encourage me ever onwards, striving towards my
true homeland.
How happy I will be to look back and say
What a life - what a journey.

Margaret Campbell

Lovers

Melt your lips upon my face
Smothered in our coiled embrace
Caress your body of sex oiled skin
Teasing at your lust within
Zones alert at loving touch
Exploding with climaxing clutch
Slowing motion of powerless thrusts
Now drained for sleep, two minds in trust
Erotic dreams of night passed by.
The lovers bond will never die.

Damien McIntyre

A Cosmic Dream

I'm lying here dreaming, dreaming in my mind,
Escaping from my body thats got me so entwined.
I'm going through the clouds, no effort is required.
      Defying all of Newtons Law like a rocket just been fired.

No up, no down, no left or right.
      Everything here is day and night.
Looking back from where I came.
      The moon is full, the earth the same.
Not hot not cold so quiet so still.
      Stars all around they shine so brill.

I journey on not knowing how far,
      The earth has just become another star.
So beautiful, so peaceful in this cosmic flight.
      So glad my mind is here tonight.

Ernie Larkin

She's the One

Unable in words or colours
I am, to do you justice,
From fine lace to floating feathers
And cool sparkling springs.

Never with imaginative gestures
Could I capture your pose,
Tall lady, small child, always
With grace and flowing femininity.

A journey through joy, the
Meaning behind those smiling blue eyes,
At times so totally captivating,
Affects my soul so beautifully, in places
Only you can reach.

Maurice Mahon

Few Thoughts

I love my home and my family, everyone father and mother,
Sisters and kin, his sisters and mother
And brothers-in-law and all.

I love in my head and my heart some special people now gone
Who colour my thoughts and my heart when I recall
A home, so big when I turned three or four
Yet later seemed to shrink as I began to grow
And notice with a wonderment of years
And comprehend what I was privileged to know.

At nine or ten my house began to change
And with sisters who strove to play and sing
And shout and swim and hop and skip and run free
I grew from temerity to reality
And I was happy really happy being one of three.

My teenage years were full of smiles and tears
And uncertainties and uncertain fears
Of clothes and records and make-up
And Saturday nights and idle chat
And stupid lonely crazy teenage things like that.

Years meant nothing then and life was carefree
Oh so clear of bother and when I met a boy I loved this boy
I felt he loved me and I didn't want to ever meet another.

But at sixteen it's hard from child to woman
To caress a silky newborn head and stare into steel blue eyes
At a son I didn't want, but with one look declared,

'I know you'll love me, you're my mother,'
And I did!

Louise Doherty

First Love

Young beech leaves in the lamplight
Rippled above my head,
Like snowflakes falling in winter
Or blossom falling in spring;
Your footsteps soft on the pavement
Echoes of my own,
Your voice clear in the lamplight
Gently piercing the darkness;
Your life walking beside mine
Whistling as we go,
Your notes floating on in the darkness
Like a tide flowing into my soul;
In years to come I shall look back and remember
And I shall never forget you.

Patricia Todd

Beneath the Stone

So here I'm lying, waiting just for you,
The stone's cold touch, in time, will thaw me through.
No sight can see the light that flickers brightly,
No sound can hear the whisper.

So now you're with me, enfolded, true,
The forms we take shall, forever bloom.
To grow together, in our secret place,
And let the stones that lie here, melt away.

Jeremy McLucas

A Memory

Day's dusk burning into night,
In a frozen field sheep huddle tight,
Thorny hedges straggling by
Branches reach to the smouldering sky.
Dark, against the crimson light
A solitary bird makes homeward flight.

Lillian E Devlin

North Atlantic Nightmare

Everybody's planning their summer holiday,
Talking about London, Paris, and LA.
They may travel every country and seek out every land,
But never find a Portrush or a Bundoran strand.

Wake up in the morning to a big greasy fry,
Toast that is burnt as black as an undertaker's tie,
Wains they are screaming, theres a hurricane outside,
Think back to your childhood, and wish that you had died.

Big fat white women who float out in the sea,
Dangerous to shipping when there's more than two or three.
Skinny little baldy man sticking out his chest,
Wishing he had muscles, wishing he was dressed.

Night-time is the right time for love and romance,
Take your little darling to disco or to dance,
Music starts to play, both get on your feet,
Get back to the table, someone's boaked upon your seat.

Where there are no beach beauties and the sun has gone to sleep,
Don't worry about the strangers, there's no-one here to meet,
For it seems your next door neighbours have followed you right here.
And the best thing about it is, it's only once a year.

Paul Taggart

Préamhaca
(roots)

I live on a green tree-bare hill
In Doire, land of oak.
In winter the lone remnant
Thrusts its branches,
Chinese brush-strokes,
Stark against the sky.

Long ago Celts hunted here.
The forests they roamed
We read of in Gaelic poetry
Writ in letters
Named of trees:
Beth - Luis - Nion.

In summer now
Children hunt the dumps.
Their plunder piled high
Burns fiercely in the night.
Limbs from saplings torn
Die to kindle the flame.
Offence to the poets
Or sacrifice to the Gods?

Sorcha Nic an tSagairt

6th Form Study

I look at you all.
You are not interested only in study.
You talk and you grin,
You defy all the rules that we made for you,
So that you could be interested only in study!

You eat childish lollipops,
It is your youth.
You come in and go out.
Some of you are attempting to work for your future,
But you bubble with life underneath.
You are young.
You are full of tomorrow.
Tomorrow you'll sit,
But to-day, on a summery morning,
You are not interested only in study.

Deirdre Devine

Jerusalem

On Friday night
From dark 'til light
Jack's jumpin'
In Jerusalem
An' wanes wi' pay
Have fish for tay
An' dance
Down in Jerusalem
Mays match is made
Bells bargain's struck
An' candles
Fit for martyrs
Stuck
In 'sticks
For lovers too
And the sentinel
Still
On the ancient hill
Curses his luck
And is blind
To their lights
Their thrills
Their pacts
Their wills
And the road to Damascus is mined.

Sean Lynch

The Waterfall

Beyond the rising spray we fall in love,
Captivated in the rushing streams
Entwined with beautiful nature, love blooms.
A love, one hope only, forever.

Hands together clutching at veils,
Spirits soar as water cascades.
Love renewed with love new born,
The secrets held within these walls of water.

Together glimpsing at the outside world,
No threats, just peace behind the storm.
If life could just remain as simple,
If love could be undying...

Memory, pure and cherished,
Behind nature's sweet aphrodisiac,
Together, arms entwined eternally
We shall watch life pass like the waterfall.

Claire Davidson

Untitled

Hailstones dancing on that cold
November day,
It was our choice to be there
In each others arms,
Watching
The storm blown waves against the
Rocks
That wild wonderful freedom of nature,
In contrast
Our wild wonderful love encaged
Yet somehow
A rainbow appeared,
Is this the sign? Is there light?
Will we one day have the freedom
To embrace?
Let our love be known.
When the storm passes will there
Still be a rainbow or just a
Cloudy sky?

Rhona Andrews

Garden

The rain falls down as soft as lace
Its sweetest touch upon my face
Our roots spread deep across the miles,
Nurtured in our dark blood while
In silent buds now all around
The gentle hopes of spring abound.

Paul McClafferty

If No-One Comes

If no-one comes
Will the dust motes breed?
What plants push fronds
Frenziedly over them to feed
On my air? I find this
Burden of light, forcing
The corners apart, persists
In spite, overpowering
All I do to salve my eyes
Assaulted by emptiness.

If no-one comes
Will the shadows meet?
What small winged irritant
Harrows the afternoon, pleating
Little sounds around the blind?
The crack in the china bleeds
Across, exploding spiderlines
To fuse wingbeat and heartbeat,
Both measuring. My blurred
Core crouches off centre.

If no-one comes
Will the dark lie down?
What worm slips against
The wood, searching round
For one crevice, just the
Right size for a wormish
Shape? I cannot push
Away. All I come up against
Are my own bones peeling.

Maura Johnston

On the Bus

She had acquired a new accent
Which she loved to display
At every opportunity
A conglomeration of Paddy, Oxford
And Yankee Doodle day.
He was verging on a complex
And Peter would have to work hard
But he can deal with it.
She knew there was a word
In answer to the clue
A fool she is and a fool she will be
Of course there was a word
Anyone could see.
And on it went postulating
Pretentious, prostituting
A twenty minute bus trip
Stretched to infinity.
She had acquired a new accent
Which she loved to display
How did she *pay*? With her soul I fear.

Aideen Devine

Twilight

Oh! to reach these twilight years,
With fast fading memories,
Bringing to mind laughter and tears,
Now all I have are fears.

Fear of the traffic,
Fear of the dark,
Fear of the dogs,
Running in the park.

Mama baked bread on the range,
As Papa filled the tin bath,
Oh! how this world has changed,
What will be the aftermath.

Gerard Craig (10)

Last Rites

Morning came,
and the cries were silent
But everybody heard them.
The poison had stroked the sunset,
now was writhing among the mind and body.
To hear the harrowing silence and the undertones of death,
and the horrid dissonance of a dial on a telephone,
as mother calls the doctor and the priest,
their message that the last had come.
Amid the malevolence of chaotic organisation,
the sorrowful ones, bereft of understanding but not of grief,
sob with bitterness and sadness.

In the hallway, a priest with oil, for anointing,
whose empty shadow casts finality in the air,
as the unearthly silence resumes its malicious tone
broken by weeping.
And I, in my early morning lethargy,
am told by some faint familiar face,
'I'm sorry son, your brother's dead.'
Too fast and beyond comprehension,
for there is no surrealism in this nightmare,
ashes to ashes, dust to dust,
from hell to heaven 'til the end,
from hell to heaven once again.

Stephen McCauley

Born Again Heroes

In the half-remembered daylight of my genesis
With hymns churning in my ears
A boy bowed in the shadowed side
Of himself at a space filled with flowers.

From that day I turned around
Banished into counsel with the damned
I saw the outcasts moving in crowds
Licking gleaming blood from their hands.

I swam away across a delirious green bay
Then lay down and slept in meadowed grass
I awoke at the footstep of the hunter's approach
And the musical craze of his laugh.

I lay under the cast and cool of his shadow dark
I froze as he grinned and drew his blade
Which blazed in the sun like redemption
I was veined with fire blood was my name.

I departed into the realms of the brotherhoods
To become a diehard hunter taught to kill
To stalk in the mind of a smile
From behind the blue gaze of a psycho Gael.

The light has gleamed about my crown
As I strode in the valleys of the heroes
I have supped with Achilles Cuchullain and Jesus
And I have never left you alone.

I moved in the fall of your shadow
Whistling the anthem of unlove
I bear the mark of a disciple
From from neither below nor above.

I am of everywhere good sir
Come and war with me anywhere.

John Harkin

Metamorphosis

Father...
Gone are your years of physical strength
The tide of Time has pounded
Relentlessly, resolutely on your life
Its language telling us
That this material cloak is ebbing, fading
Your body like a fallen autumn leaf
Crisp and dry, now subject to the whispering wind
That will take it away to decompose
Yet out of this spent matter
Blossoms forth a delicate flower
Fresh, precious - emerging from the spirit
Like a bead of rain attracting a passing ray of light
Sparkling fleeting moment of beauty
Now noticed by the family
From which each one becomes involved
And in that caring moment
Seeds of Compassion, Patience, Thoughtfulness
Conceive and bring forth blooms
That are recognised and in return
The spring of yet another harvest
Blossoms with Appreciation, Gratitude
And in this interchange
Each one is blessed and given
Yet another chance to re-discover
The true meaning of
Family.

Gladys Mulligan

The Amethyst Hills

From the amethyst hills on wings of silk,
Clouds sail beneath the brilliance of a
Turquoise sky.
And stencilled in the eastern light
The span of an eagle's wing in flight.

Eyes of black pebble stare out of the sand
Of centuries, and in the distance
The whisper of the cobalt sea.

When the artist sees the rainbow,
He fades the light with a brush stroke,
And stabs the canvas with his palette knife.

Rosaleen Clarke

Vows

With dreams of love
You caught me, ensnared with
Rings of gold.
Romantic, silken threads tightened
Held me fast
Unfree.
From a captive body
You freely drank
A swollen belly your ownership claimed
Always wanting - not unkind
You turn your back as I offer you
My bewildered mind.

Una Walsh

Baking

When I was young I stood beside my mother
        as she baked the bread.
'Use spotless hands, don't be afraid
        to cut the Cross on top,' she said.

'Since bread was baked on stones,' she taught,
        'Women have crossed the dough,
Have prayed unspoken prayers that men come home,
        that ways are safe and children fed.'

So now I mix the dough for mine
        with shaking hands and guilty heart
And though I don't believe in God
        I draw His cross, I play the part.

Though Christ lies broken through the land
        I make his imprint in the dough
For reasons I don't understand
        and unknown women.

Ann Keith-Sandford

A Loved One So Dear

Black misery, brown coffin,
Crowded and smoke filled rooms
A white ashen face sleeping peacefully
Joined hands holding a pair of beads.

Lying there so peaceful
We wonder where her soul lies
Is it as peaceful as she
Or is it crying out for mercy.

We thank them for their sympathy
They thank us for our tea
'You'll get over it dear'
They will but never, never me.

The silence in her room
She and I together for the last time
I speak to her and watch her face
Hoping one day we will speak again.

They close the coffin lid
Never to be unlocked
Never to be disturbed
The pain and agony - set free?

Anita Jackson

The Voyage of Brendan
(for Louise)

In the jewel of the night
you bring a baby out
and there's no mystery
in it

but tiredness
and a brutal birth
take home an empty womb.

Yet waters broke
and Brendan is apart,
drinking up the myth,
sparkling like a pebble
in the heat,
signalling your belief
in brilliant life.

His eyes roll
like the sea circling your world -
now welcoming,
now dark -
fixing the contradictions
in the gentle eye
of your storm.

So let the voyage start.

Lawrence Price

The Dangerous Hobbies of Johnny Blackbeard MP

Order Order
Lets not bother about our poor mother's
They're old and cost money
And their nappies need changing
And lets not bother about our father's fodder
Greenhouses are much better nowadays.

Lets not bother
And lets not forget
About all those who oppose us
Right honourable gentry lads
Oh! that would be improper

Now we'll sleep all day
For a good wage
And feed on gin and sage
At the expense of our lessors

'Here, Here,' Mr Speaker
It is unanimous.

Thomas I Maguire

The Mouse

When I'm by myself and reading
When I've cut myself and bleeding
I hear you

When I'm in the bathroom singing
Or when birds go softly winging
I hear you

When the clock the hour is chiming
And the second hand is timing
I hear you

When I'm in my bed for sleeping
I can hear you as you're creeping
Constant scratching, constant eating
Little mouse, I'll get you.

James Coyle

Silences

And, sometimes now, silences doze between us.
Soft, gentle stills that are content to gather thought-filled dust,
but are dismissed by an ugly, useless word.

They are the finest silences that I have never heard.

And, other times, silences wake between us.
Awkward, empty lulls that expand and rot like rust,
But are dispelled by a simple, saving word.

They are the longest silences that I have yet endured.

Nicholas Laird

Circle

Pounding on the keyboard of reality, I look to see that, as always,
there are mistakes.
So much for the two-fingered typist. The two fingered gesture.
Bloodstains on the door and on our knuckles as we try to find that
elusive paradise but instead find turmoil.
All the quasi-religious hypocrisy and nationalism, rolled up in a ball
which sticks in the throat.
Rain and rosary beads will not diffuse the disillusionment or the
resentment in a country divided by prejudice.
With surrender comes coercion, without it aggression.
From one man to the masses, the line goes on,
A never ending circle.

Liam Porter

Grey Point in June

Wild bees and bluebells,
Badgers and black rabbits;
Skylarks and sycamore trees,
Giant rhubarb and bramble flowers;
Orange and yellow honey bees
in the wisteria.

Golden rays of the evening sunlight
Sparkle to the waters edge,
Where sea pinks nestle among the rocks.
The elderflower spreads its lacy blossoms,
towards the flecked sky;
Everything is humming and then silent -
Before the on coming storm.

Kathleen Baillie

Derry

The calmness of the city
Like impending doom, settles on
The deserted streets.
Boarded windows, shattered buildings
Where no birdsong or creature
Can be heard.
The sadness of it all
Compels not tears -
For the broken hearts and
Wasted lives,
Have long since been buried
In the debris of the passing years.
The writing on the wall
Will be their epitaph -
There is no tombstone big enough
To tell their tale.

Mary Josephine Devlin

Earth Matters

She hovers unyielding
Changed yet unchanging
Her past victorious
Her future uncertain
How many generations have said
We're the best ever?
How many generations *must* say
We hang our heads in shame?
We seem to learn more
Every Era
But mother earth
Takes a step back
Time is of an essence
But how endless is time?

L V Wilson

A Sonnet to Mozart

How oft, immortal Mozart, did I mourn
Thy poor unhappy lot to contemplate;
That shamefully to common grave was borne
Your little mortal body in a heap
With half a score of corpses which like thee
Shared death, a resting place and few to weep.
Yet why should I regret what was to be?
What matter that no headstone mark the spot,
No scrolléd epitaph or chiselled date,
Nor iron rails to guard the sacred plot?
Thy music is a monument which Time -
The truest critic yet of Art or Man -
Has proved more durable, more age-secure,
Than boldest architect had dared to plan.

J A Sinton

Easter Roulette

The devil took a chance,
One last despairing dance
Of death or victory complete.
He'd killed the prophets, stoned their sons,
Dispersed his lies in clever cons.
Sure in sardonic pride he drew
His sword of hate, and Christ he slew.
Swinging the trigger on his thumb,
He felled his victim. Battle won!
'Twas victory hurranica
For Lucifer Satanica!
Then whence this stone rolled clean away?
These shining Beings' bright array?
The cloth from off the Corpse's face
Cast carelessly beside the place
Where He had lain?
Vital! Alive! There stands the Man
Whom he had slain,
Christ risen again!
The hand that held hell's gambling tub
Belonged to dark Beelzebub.
God's was the hand the dice had tossed,
And Satan lost...

Win Harwood

Orogeny

When something new reaches for the sun
even the core of a mountain is moved
for the merest atom-seed of life
runs in our race also
and each new heart
is welcomed over the finish line

Yet not all is glory and rejoicing
more a confirmation of faith
like the tears encouraged by childbirth
as if to say yes
it is true
mountains can be moved

Séan Greer

Solitude

Dear lonely, beautiful moon,
How solemn and calm you look!
Sailing all alone, in your sea
Of solitude.
Share with me my friend, the
secret of your survival, the
beauty of your ways,
Wreathed in shadows which
pass you by.

All alone, high above in the
Black night sky,
You loom, pale as death,
Strange, yet compelling,
To the curious eye
Of a passer-by.
Lonely, yet contented to gaze
at glistening stars.
An inspiration to so many, yet
visited by so few.

A M Chambers

And then the Frost

Bleak night,
in prison hills
abound with concrete towers
and then the frost.

Bitter silence,
in Irish homes
among the living, the stench of death
and then the frost.

Tunnel vision,
in many minds
within our hearts, the answer lies
and then the frost.

Maureen Smyth

The Little I Keep

On my back flimsy and sodden she rode.
Animal game sassed from cat and mouse horseplay.
Uppity I canter across this the carpet.
Eyes standing in my neighbours face, floodlit
For all like Spanish castle cathedrals.

Tremble thimble, prick-proof and beyond the
darting ball of fur we call this welcome face.

One two three red-lights and lobsters, mobsters
and slobsters.

Daniel Spencer Harley

Alpha and Omega

The last day of the year
All is quiet, all is still
Fire flickers in the grate
Sounds from the box in the corner
Comes brash and bright.

Memory flashes back
To New Year's Eve of old
Bustle of cooking
Smells that tickle the nostrils.

Everything ready,
Will he come?
Headlights appear, car door bangs
A smiling face comes around the door

All is well
Sit and listen to the New Year bells
Drink a health to the coming year.

Alas, those days have gone
A meal for one by the fireside is utmost
Where has Alpha and Omega gone?

Joan Crossan

Time

Time to get up
time to go to bed
time to wash up
time to be fed
time is of the essence
there's a time and place
time and time again
a wound time can't erase
when your time is up
there's no time to say no
no time for goodbye
just time to go

Michael Beare

Story to a Young Daughter

'I will tell you a story of the longships with the high carved prows,
And storms at sea and battles...'
'Not that one, Daddy, another.'
'Then I'll tell of foreign wars and tanks and planes,
And heroes made of iron...'
'You told me that last night.'
'Well, then, I'll talk of children in a magic land,
Protected, almost, by a wizard's spell...'
'Not that one, Daddy, - tell the story of the Lord of Time.'

'I will, then, listen, for the words are soft,
And, if you miss them, they might not come back.
I will tell you of a time when one man only walked the earth.
One man who met a girl of shining beauty, and of swinging hair -
Yes, dear, she looked a lot like you -
The clock stood still at summertime and they, -
They walked together through the warm green grass.
She was the summer sun, and when he held her hand,
He was the Lord of Time, and no one else
Existed in that magic land of love, and they were
Strong and beautiful...'
'Why, Daddy, are you crying?'
'Hush, dear, listen
To the ticking of the clock,
See how the night draws on.'

G Wills

War and Peace

Love thy neighbour
Tramp, tramp
Love thy enemy
Tramp, tramp, tramp
Do good to those who hate you
Blazing gun fire
Pray for those who persecute you
Tramp, tramp; blazing gun fire;
Be compassionate
Ambulance sirens
Do not judge
Accusing political speeches
Do not condemn
Accusing political speeches; Ambulance sirens;
Pardon
Coffin lowered
Give
Flowers for the dead
Coffin lowered
Flowers for the dead
And it will be given to you...

Ethna Johnston

False Justice

I lie there,
Thinking,
Thinking about where Justice is now,
At a time like this,
Some Justice!
Accused of what I did not do,
And sent down.

I feel betrayed,
Where now is the one I worship?
But then what do I expect?
All evidence against me,
Even I would have convicted me,
But all I now feel is hatred,
A hatred of those who would not believe.

Now I know how mice feel,
Trapped and innocent,
With no way out,
Sure,
They feed me,
But what did I do?
What but nothing,
Nothing at all.

Why is there no Justice
For those who look guilty?
'Never judge a book by its cover',
But where is that now?
All there is,
Is False Justice,
And innocence branded guilty.

James Jackson (14)

Perfect Union

When the model was earthed the electrode
Stroked the cold, unyielding metal
Exploding the darkness of the studio
At the moment of contact.

Instantly the arc was formed
The metals began to flow, fusing
Into each other to form a single
Body born of the searing heat.

As the rod burned down and the arc
Was broken darkness returned
While the ticking metal cooled
After the electrode's discharge.

When we were earthed
I caressed your cold unyielding body
Until sparkling into perfect union
Then the heartbeat of sated passion.

Sean McWilliams

Self Destruction

It is evil
This worm inside
This need to destroy
To devour all that is good

A fraction of a second
A hair-breadth of time
Before the milk turns sour
The apple bad

This need emerges
Driving a path
Looking neither to left or right
Intent obsessively on destruction

Signals have registered
The approach of one who might
Break through the self-erected barrier
Protecting a fragile put-together heart

Channels of communication to the brain
Translate the code - danger is close
He might invade that precious place
He might touch the real you

Mary Carson

Childhood Friend

Standing alone in the playground
She watched her friend draw near
He was old and grey and crumpled
But to her was very dear
He told her funny stories
Above the playground noise
And sometimes gave out sweeties
To special girls and boys
Billy's job ensured
He was never far away
She laughed when he called her Goldilocks
And cuddled her each day
He was her one and only friend
She trusted him completely
And when she sat upon his knee
He spoke to her so sweetly
He said she was a good girl
But she must never tell
Of how when Billy touched her
It made his trousers swell.

Jacqueline McGregor

Dispossession

Layer upon layer of hurt and pain lie smouldering
beneath this facade of normality - ready to erupt
at any given time - like violence on a hot muggy urban
street in summer.

The paper over the joins is straining at the seams and
must surely give birth to these imprisoned thoughts.
Deep in the subconscious a voice over and over again
repeats -

All the wasted moments,
All the empty days,
All the unlived fantasies,
Are the total of our days.

All the places never visited,
All the words we never said,
All the thoughts unuttered,
Are the total of our ways.

The festering continues and with each new pain increases.
Churning over, ready to be released.

Sharon McCleery

Artemis Dream Forgotten

Love amidst tenderest bloom
Immortal life
the sacred womb
Alas like vapour
tis past so soon
Sensual nature
We ascribe to a tomb
the valley
the shadow
the rider on a pale horse loom's
A dwelling appointed for all living -
A tomb.

Raymond Dinsmore

Here

M1 *Carbine*
SLR
Armalite
Armoured car
Bottle green jackets and camouflage.
RPG
Proxy bomb
Where are ye comin' from?
Where are ye goin'?
Batons and black balaclavas
Hi-jacked buses
Burnt out wrecks
Flying Tri-colours and Union Jacks
Red hands, shamrocks, harps and crowns.
Rebels
Grand Masters
Taig and Orange bastards
Apart from that it's alright here.

Kevin Meehan

A Quiet Place

The mountains were present
Watching always
Reverberated:
Fingers reaching up to them
Like voices -
The last children playing
In the street.

Hard cow-dung from yesterday
Furrowing the narrow
Road:
Touched by an early frost
Clear as an eye -
A circle of nothing, like blood
On the soil.

Crumpled like a sack
All but naked
Silent:
Hands tied behind back
Head hooded -
This morning, the school bus will go
A different way.

Gary Allen

Impressions

Breakfast tables in empty rooms
Unmade beds in the afternoon
Quiet days when thunder looms
And all good things that end too soon.

Dusty parlours looking onto quiet streets
Bedrooms that still smell of sleep
Washrooms full of linen sheets
And all good things that I've failed to keep.

The smell of wood smoke and new cut lawns
Winter nights and frosty dawns
Memories of you now you're gone
Keep me from moving on.

Joseph Allen

A Season's Touch

I am a gift from The Lord on high,
Bestowed on a still, dark earth.
My voice awakens the sleeping eye
And my touch is the soil's rebirth.

Each year begins with my season's role.
I command the birds to sing.
On nature's stage my words extol.
I am the stirring voice of spring.

With a power of strength within my hand
Beyond the wildest dreams,
I can unlock the frozen rivers and,
Set free the icebound streams.

I arrange soft buds upon the trees.
I dress elms, oaks and willows.
Then my breath becomes a scented breeze
In the forests and the hollows.

I move swiftly through some fairy glen.
I colour mountains, valleys, hills,
Create the tiny snowdrops, then
I gild the early daffodils.

I am newborn lambs at gentle play.
I am birds high on the wing.
I am first, fresh light of each new day.
I am the season God named spring.

Theresa Rafferty

For Yorick: Late August

Like much that is best in life you came by chance
My Yorick, my 'fellow of infinite jest'.
Picture the scene! A blustery Saturday
Afternoon - a busy road with brisk traffic
toing
and
froing.
Late August; four o'clock or was it nearer
Half past the hour? A sudden, fleeting glimpse of
Smallness and blackness on a traffic island.
Stopping, retracing, a second look revealed
you.
Perched with solemn wandering eyes and skimpy
Lustreless coat. Yet your response was friendly.
Unafraid, with tail erect you made your way
straight
towards me.

I thought of bones, crushed bones and hollowed eyeless
Skulls, whilst you, so innocently unaware
Began to purr and nestle happily close,
Allowing me to rescue you from almost
Certain death that special August afternoon.

J C Nelson

Magic

Subdued light falls gently
upon your manuscripts,
you sit below the window

with the pages of your story
scattered as you shape and cut
with ink a truth, your truth.

The children are asleep
you sit silent smoking
a roll your own cigarette,

You can almost hear it
the river that runs through
the council estate,
the cities,
the countries,
the pure water.

Outside stationary cars rusting,
empty streets, a wind growing stronger
threat of rain

you lift your pen
and begin to write.

John Corvan

November Admiral

'A butterfly emerges from a darkened closet,
bringing a burst of summer to a pale shallow room.
An expectant father strides in circles, like the
butterfly patrolling a naked light-bulb.
Yet the moment is still not at hand!
For the butterfly the artificial heat has brought
summer too soon, for the expectant parents the
stillborn silence has brought the shadow of death.
The butterfly retreats to the closet, the would-be
parents sit grief-stricken and alone.'

John McCabe

A Winter Zoo

Summon the children, that they may learn
the thresholds of an intemperate climate,
to climb these icy steps, this fence-crossed hill,
that they may come to know keeper and cage.

While predators lie safe, the children run at risk,
pallid eyes betray their cares
and wishes, that avenues and parks
may lead from here, this discontent.

Call a roll of absent animals
in hibernation from the hunt and shoot,
recognise this as the province of cold blood
where trenched canals lie locked in ice.

By snare or trap, the cages are laid open,
the invitation is to step inside
where sleep is wilful, dreams run slow.
Come join your order in the winter zoo.

Arthur Campbell

Untitled

Hindu, Muslim, Christian Sikh
Mosque and temple, bangles and Baksheesh
Roads and streets and excavations
urination defecation
Taxi, rickshaw, bus and train
baggage, bodies, take the strain.
Sunrise, sunset, damned mossy pest
never rest see Everest
Gandhi, Nehru, Place to stay?
Namas De and how you pay?
Sacred cows and goats and camels
Silver, marble, brass and enamels
Delhi station, mass occupation
lepers, cripples, near starvation
Loreto nuns and Gurkas guns
stinking loo, got the runs
Dollars, pounds, crores of rupees
diarrhoea dysentery
Dioralyte and flagyl pills
Delhi belly, here's your bill
Ghats and bats and rats and cats
Silks and saris, shawls and Tibetan hats
Taj Mahal, Masala dal
Dali Lama, cricket ball
Lotus flower and Mogul Art
India hopeless, helpless heart.

T P McNamee

Belfast Telegraph

Front page news,
misnomer extraordinary,
recalling other days, weeks, years,
reads:

RUC investigates the murders
of retired vicar and his daughter
in Cookstown on 15th December '92,
he battered to death, her eye stabbed through;

Shots fired at cabbie near Lurgan
miss this time,
leaving one unmurdered victim
and another unsolved crime;

Bomb hoax chaos choking rush-hour traffic
on the Sydenham By-pass in Belfast,
the early morning standstill
a microcosm of the place;

Burton Group announces job cuts
sweetened with a promise -
'key-time' posts for full-time jobs -
in the ratio of three to one;

Further cheer is proffered, January only,
by a Belfast travel agency
reducing summer package holidays
in exchange for unused Hoover products.

So today's news ripples slowly
across the surface
of this deep, stagnant pool:
Ulster.
Joseph Boucher

The Word

The master flexes his foil,
The deadly arrow strikes home,
An Einstein of dictation
Limbers the sharpening stone,
'Nothing to chance,'
A very amiable pursuit.

'Pary' et 'Pary' rehearsed,
The dagger of subliminal structure,
A wolf amid a vast emptiness of tedium,
A conversation one million thoughts old.

Desmond Durkan

Growing Old with the Day

A wondrous sunrise to a new life,
The nurturing morning warms the body
A babe rolls in its cot,
the early morning comes rolling in.
The first steps of the day watches,
in awe of a child's steps.
The sun watches the child from afar
life begins to speed up.
A second dawning as maturity
catapults life out of the old ways,
Into a new arena.
The light of the day guides us into the future.
As the light dulls a family gather round,
An extinguishing night puts out the
dim candle ready to be re-lit.
But tomorrow brings new life with another sunrise.

Liam Quigley (15)

Sacrifice

The restless orange oak-leaves blustered round
in sorrow; slanting sleet turned ash and dust
to muck, eroding too the dug out mound
of earth, eroding tears of those who must
be seen to mourn. But Uncle Davy watched.
In big red hands his tearless face nestled
against the wretched pain that was unmatched,
and yet he stood alone, peripheral.

I called on him the night before I left.
His mother dead four years, and still he lays
the table-cloth with butter dish and blessed
the milk jug, and at this altar always prays.
And silently there in her memory,
we buttered bread and drank the holy tea.

Niall Grimes

Old House in Tamlaghtmore

The empty windows: the broken slates.
The dark dank smell of long past life:
The blue sky through broken beams,
The gentle wind: a breath of dreams.

Where are you who stood at the door
The distant hills to scan no more?
The stitchwort blooms in the ancient hedge
And the ivy coils around the sycamore.

No more the laughter and the tears
Of life in those long-gone years.
A wee bird wings as it did then
And the fox is sleeping in his den.

As you sleep beneath the stars,
Man of the soil and toil of years.
The seagulls cry over the upturned drill
But for you the tender earth is still.

Thomas Spiers

The Craft of the Hermaphrodite

The poet writes to celebrate the shadow
And yet the true soul,
He affiliates the demonic
With the daimonic
In the hope of resolution;
The innately mundane
And spiritual union.

He becomes the god
Of self-created reality
And yet,
Like the Nazarene prophet,
Walks the path of man.

He is the final arbiter
Of the mystic and the magical,
The transcendent visionary
Whose words become manifest
In Kether and Tiphareth.

Sweet realisation,
From the lips of a madman.

Simon D Leeman

The Glories of War

I saw the children in the bomb-blitzed street,
With jaundiced skin and hungry eyes,
No bed to sleep in, no bread to eat,
Their lives destroyed by politicians lies.

I heard the wail of an abandoned child,
No mother to care for her, 'another mouth to feed',
One of nature's outcasts, by life reviled,
Her hope torn apart by an arms-dealer's greed.

I smelt the smoke from the bomb-blitzed flat,
Love and warmth were once there; long now vacated,
The mortar-bombs made sure of all that,
Launched and paid for by bigots hatred.

I felt the anguish this conflict had dealt,
The screams of lost orphans rang out through the night,
I saw, I heard, I smelt, I felt,
The glories of war - what a hideous sight.

David Rogers

Peanuts - Crisp, Dry Yet Salty

Can I smooth your
Dry skin
Peal off your past
And bring to where
You are no more,
Mass produced.
Your life drained from
Within delicate veins
You leave my lips
Sore, salt stains,
My taut tissue
You are crisp
Once dry
Yet ever so
(Salty) beautiful.

Paul Kelly

Himself

I just take him for granted
He is always there you see
But he knows how much I love him
And I know that he loves me.

We argue about the buildings
And we argue about our sons
And we argue about this and that
And the way things should be done.

He doesn't win all the battles
I win quite a few
And sometimes we agree to differ
And go on to something new.

Our life it is exciting
And we have a lot of fun
But here is also some tough times
And hard work to be done.

Sometimes things run smoothly
Sometimes everything goes wrong
But it is at times like this
That our love is very strong.

As we go through life together
For everyone to see
I know that I can cope with everything
If this man is here with me.

Lil Brady

To Break a Butterfly...

Your brutality
Awakens my brutality
Your cold black eyes
Darken my joy
Your body tenses
Mine stiffens
Your grasping hand
Finds no love to clutch to.

Rhoda Quinn

A View From the Sky

Through the white, wispy clouds,
I caught my first glimpse,
A sight familiar,
A feeling renewed,
The green fields,
Partitioned by hedges,
The beautiful landscape,
With twisting rivers,
Isolated houses, farms,
Lakes, forests, hills,
Everything... *Ireland.*

The first glimpse,
Belies every vision, dream,
You ever had of it,
Totally fulfilling, expanding,
The stereotypical image,
It fills your heart,
With awe,
Such a contrast in appearances,
To the land just departed,
Distance veils the troubles
The magnet draws,... *Ireland.*

Nicola Doherty

Untitled

Silence is enforced
From the
Turbulent corridor
Edged with passions
And mishaps
Passions so passionate
And mishaps so
Desperate, there was
Nothing left but
Silence
But silence being
Silence leaves
Behind it immortality.
And it is this
Immortality for which
I live.

R Griffin

My Mournes

The mountains of Mourne, they captivate me,
With their dark majestic beauty
As they sweep down to the sea.

Other mountains I have gazed on ,
Much higher by far,
But they were not my Mournes,
So I shed a silent tear.

Sleve Donard, Sleve Bernagh, Sleve Bignian.
Their names are sweet music
To an exile like me.

Your valley so silent, so silent up there,
With its clear crystal water
That mean life to men.

If only one goblet of this I could drink,
I would raise it high and say,
'Slainte' and 'Slainte' again.

Emily Bronte Taylor

The Literary Maiden's Lament or
Men I Just Couldn't Marry and One I could

I couldn't marry a solicitor,
They have no conscience;
I couldn't live with that.
Nor a banker,
Coming home every day
Having to say,
I evicted three widows,
And seventeen children to-day.
No, that's not my way.

Or a doctor;
They are too insensitive,
Too frustrated,
Too tired!

And what about policemen?
Well, I mean to say,
Who would insure them?
And what good's that to me
When I have to bury one.
No, leave well alone!

I won't even mention soldiers!

Rather, give me a man,
Who'll come home from a hard day's work
To a house full of dirty dishes, and clean and hoover bags,
Look wondrously at the little poem
I have agonized over since breakfast,
And lovingly say,

'Darling! did you really do all this to-day?'
To which I shall smile shyly,
Totally ignoring the mess
And proudly reply, 'Yes.'
And we'll both live happily ever after!

Myra Dryden

Madame Butterfly on the Terrace

Madame Butterfly on the terrace
Sing sweet,
Sing low,
And weave the night together, blackest velvet
Cover for lovers entwined in sweet union
-ungodly desire.
Woman - holds tight to the scent that
                               wrapped him
-Lingering, stale
-Yesterday's memories
A single rose and a card, poor commission
                               cast on the stand.
Chocolate eyes - 'Drink me in,' they said
She drowned in her longing.

Sing sweet,
Sing low,
One day, he'll return.

Claire Marie Norris

Fond Memories

These I have loved,
Silver grey horses dappled with white,
The cool of the evening; the still of the night,
Sparkling blue eyes, long flowing hair,
Ripe juicy strawberries, the noise of a fair,
A blanket of snow, by humans untouched,
All of these things, I have loved so much.

Trina Porter

Synthetic Reality

Somewhere a darkness is waiting
To steal the light from the skies
Somewhere an army is threatening paradise
Somewhere a nation is starving
And slowly dying away
Somewhere a government dreams of yesterday.

But here am I
In a world of unreality
Conditioned to look for
What I'm allowed to see.

Somewhere a wind will be blowing
And gently turning the tide
Someday an answer will surely be supplied
Somewhere a war that is raging
Denotes the ending of trust
Somewhere a saviour is rising from the dust.

But here am I
In a world of unreality
Conditioned to look for
What I'm allowed to see.

Ken Grimason

Up Spake the Champion

Up spake the champion to all the little hens,
Is not chess all physiological,
And replied this little hen,
Clucking out an offering to his mother,
Just look at the games of Capablanca,
Grin split face, eyes blazing,
What a clever little dickey bird.

Add knowledge,
Do not add understanding,
And you get brainwashed little hens,
Taking pleasure in talking garbage to their mothers.

Ken Adams

Which Way?

From the deck I gaze:
Far out.
The stiff sea breeze;
Clears my mind,
Ruffles my thoughts,
Tangles my hair.

A door slams shut:
A tinge of sadness settles.
Startled by sudden change,
Which way?
To Scotland perhaps -
Or elsewhere.

Cora Cassidy

A Love Poem

He said, ' Write something about me now,'
Putting on his breadwinner's face.
I smiled and felt quite flattered at this sudden recognition.

But how does one avoid gushing sentiment
When writing of the one you love?
Do I say, 'You are my sun my moon my stars,
You shelter me from the knocks and disappointments
Life has to offer?'

Or simply that your folding of warm damp towels
Has always puzzled me?

Muriel Cameron

Essence

Take time to know me: *Really* know me.
Find out who I am: who I want to be.
Ask me where I'm going: where I want to go.
Discover my nuances, that, that makes me, *Me:*

And when you've found me: love me.
Cherish my individuality: revel in my joys,
Console me when I cry; believe in me -
(sometimes when I don't believe in myself) -
Trust in me, nurture in me *Your* hopes, your dreams.

Enshrine in me your future: all that you are,
All that you hope to be.
Strive for that goal - so beyond your reach alone:
Yet so attainable together!

Love me, cherish me, care for me -
For it is your being which makes me great.

Marleen Rajan

Pecking Order

Minus 2, and freezing.
Fat-bellied vultures
Descend from red buses
Onto Kensington High Street
To peck the fertile ground
For Christmas worms.

Blind as bats,
They do not see
The face of Jesus
On the pavement
Outside Marks and Spencer;
Or pause to read his sign
No Food, No Money, Please Help.

Round at Lincoln's Inn Fields
They are tearing down
His cardboard stable.
And tomorrow, he will add
Homeless to his greeting card.

Bernie McClelland

Emotions

Crowded church,
Heads bowed
Some sniffle
Others sob
Sermon over
Silence
Shoulders twitch
All stand
Feet shuffle
Bells chime
Heads raised high
Chorus of singers
Break into song.

Kathleen Canville

Loneliness

In a cold city,
In a cold town,
In a cold street,
In a cold house,
In a cold room,
Sat an old lonely lady.

No money for her hungry meter,
No light to guide her way,
This lady was not cold before her friends let go,
This lady was not cold before.

Despair lurked in every cold, dark corner,
And slowly, very, very, slowly,
This lady passed away.

Gráinne McCay

Arrival at the Factory

Hills shrouded by low cloud
Gulls screaming in anticipation
Of scraps of unwanted food
Thrown out by overfed humans.

Distant sounds of machinery
Penetrating shells of steel and concrete
Disturbing Natures' peaceful scene
But essential to man's ego and survival.

Dawn has changed to brightness
Clouds scatter and lift from the hills
As if drawn by magnets in the sky above
Patches of pale blue proclaim a brighter day.

Unseen from the outside in their honeycombs
Humans, mindful of their basics, toil and sweat
Oblivious to the changing elements outside their sphere
Aware of the necessity to work and live.

The day lengthens amid changing scenes
The shift has finished it seems
Men make their way to exits in the hive
Inhale fresh air, give thanks in silent prayer.

Gilbert N Thorpe

Woman vs Woman

Yes, I'm the 'other woman'
An ugly fact, but true.
I'm the one who loves him
All the time he's not with you.

I wait for hurried phone calls,
Stolen time, but oh, so sweet!
Those tender times we spend
Together make me feel complete.

He phones from work and from the bar,
We talk and scheme and plan.
To me, he is my everything,
To you, he's just 'your man'.

I hate you for owning him,
He's happier with me.
But duty binds him to you,
My loving sets him free.

I'm left with precious thoughts for him,
And a bed that's suddenly cold.
You get him back - but do you?
Do you know the man you hold?

I am his fantasy, his lover, his joy,
You represent boredom and coldness.
I know all his inner thoughts,
You know nothing of his boldness.

I'll always be in his memory,
He will always think of me.
His presence may be with you,
But I have his heart, you see.
Geraldine McIlmurray

Cherry Blossom

One May morning I saw the sprightly dancer
Gliding to and fro
Silhouetted against a sky of mottled blue
Staged on a solitary bough.

The dawn pink petalled figure balanced
Swayed, and bowed gracefully
Rustling breeze propelling the whole display
I stood transfixed.

Every morning for a week or more I watched
That same performance from curtain-up
To encore, until one sudden dawn
I looked and she was gone.

Anne Cairns

Northern Ireland (1993)

It's raining limbs again today.
On the street lies a carpet of blood.
Twisted torso's mutely hang
From a weeping willow tree.
Fractured faces dumbly float
Upon the crimson sea.

Weeping wounded wander,
Agony etched in empty faces.
Warped words escape
From a bloody, hollow cave.
Silently praying that the pain may pass,
Silently craving a comforting grave.

Norah Brown

Night Shifts

Four oh eight in the shifting,
From dark to dawn. The night
Filled with nothing. I breathe.
No spoon shaped shared pairings
Beneath the blanketed warmth.
No soft sure sense of you;

Without which I am lost,
Adrift, on a solitary tide. Clasping
Knees to chest, I hold on, foetus-like
To some singular reality. I breathe again.
The darkness shifts with each halation,
As if it were a part of it too.

These vulnerable moments, when faith
Faces the void, weighted,
Thought filled sounds, lie unbearably close
To the shores of unreason.
I shiver, I breathe.

Jim Davidson

On Buying a Poinsettia

Go on buy it, break the mould
Shatter her illusion of you.
What matter if she mocks
Spurns into the red heart of the thing
With closed eyes and mind.
Look, it draws you
Back for a second look.
The green leaves, but mostly
The blood flowers.
Their brightness upsets you
Bringing back a tumble of feelings
You thought long dead.
Her, could she see it?
Go on, it's worth the risk.
Buy it.
Take it boldly home
And confront her with it.

Sandra Elwood

Life

I lie here thinking
Of what my life could have been,
Of the towns and the cities
That I've never seen,
Of the peace in the country
Full of mountains and lakes,
And the beautiful swan and the
Music it makes.

Live life to the fullest
Is what I've been told,
Enjoy your days now
If it's warm, if it's cold,
The time soon will come
When you reach my age,
Confined to a bed -
Like a bird in a cage.

So now I have told you
Of what you must do,
Believe me my young ones
I know it is true,
So do not feel sorry
For one's own mistakes,
Live life to the fullest
And enjoy what it makes.

Richard Wilson

The Preacher Man

I passed him, looking like a drowned
Rat in the rain. He was shouting.
All I managed to catch in the echo
Was 'Washed in the blood.'
I looked at him stupidly, more in
Wonder and disbelief.
I was trying to get home, on a
Bloody wet day and I think he was
Trying to get to a drier one,
Somewhere in the clouds.

The rain started to beat down
Heavier now, as if messages were
Coming from above as well.
This made him shout louder and
The words 'Redeemed' ran through
My head.
What did this all mean?
He was long out of sight and I
Could still hear him chanting,
No doubt looking deep into the
Eyes of some other wet sod who
Passed him by in the rain.

Maggie Mayberry

Faded

Born of Green,
In soft Atlantic seas.
Glowing red,
Painful skin and place,
In times of change and anger,
The colours change.

Orange falls,
By force of bitter green fruit,
Things to change,
In a land of slow war dying.
Wash their hands,
Alone to face the music, changed.

Scarlet Red,
A danger to myself and others,
All talk,
Talking red of change,
Faded,
By time and the times, changed.

Dusty Pink
A softer shade of angry.
Things to change,
Starting now with me,
Choice,
To run or stay forever, faded.

Soft sea green,
A mask to hide the rainbow.
Stir it up,
Just because I can.
Chameleon,
All to all, all faded, changed.
Michael Hegarty

By the Seaside

Quiet lap of waves against the silver sand.
Quiet fall of eve when all is still
The glassy shimmer of the sun reflects the sky
A sky that makes the hills seem nearer still.

The restless bats come out to feed on wing
Above the patient fishermen in boats
Who cast their nets and creels with fervent hope
That on the morrow they may find them full.

The dawn comes up the sun climbs in the sky
The gulls and terns the noisy birds they are
Devour their unsuspecting prey with ardent relish
And feed their fledgling young on ledge and crevice.

Warm sunny day with haze on hills and water
Kintyre misted out but Garron still in view
The village slowly wakes
Familiar noises rend the air
The clang of anvil from the smithy
The bell that calls the workmen to their toil.

Soon we hear blast in nearby quarry
The rumble of laden carts upon their way
To spill their loads of limestone
Into the boat thats tied up at the quay.

Children laugh and play at the seashore
Church clock chimes the passing hours away
Men and boy gather in the farmyard
To have a game of football
Or argue and debate the topic of the day.
A village is a perfect place to grow up in
Where memories are etched forever on the mind.
John McGowan

Moonrise

The moon rose out of the water
As a bright and golden orb.
The black outline of her mountains
Conceptually absorbed
My mind, as I paused and wondered
On the man who used to be
Up there, on the lunar summits
Or set in the tranquil sea.

This fascinating object
Which used to bind a spell,
Has now lost all its mystery,
The moonmen rang the knell.

Richard Ross

Untitled

Who can put their thoughts on paper
And say 'This is right'?
Without remorse and criticism
From self and others
Who is it that stands out amongst averageness?
Yet is it their right to say
Who can put down? And yet
Never know the right is theirs
What one feels can it be assured?
Ignorance, why give scorn to those who have nothing
But meagre ways.
Why not?
It is not their excuse, They are
Ignorant of their
Ignorance, they swim in euphoric pools of nothing.

But those who praise and speak of rarity, I hate,
I loathe, their thoughts, their views
Bastards! Why should I listen to them?
Their dirt, their opinions, their perverted
Sense of great and greatness
Must I listen, must I despise, must I see the
Frailty of their words?
Who is it that stands out?
But hesitates
Is it me?

Richard McLaughlin

Untitled

They'll shatter the dreams
Of a million young parents
Trying to give their child a life
Mothers, Fathers, who worry from conception onwards,
Is my child safe? Is my child sleeping?
They'll shatter the dreams.

See the baby laugh, smile, play
See the baby sleep.
And think
Can one man kill the happiness
The happiness that has been cried out for
The happiness that we live for
Is it fair that one man has the power to destroy this?

They'll shatter the dreams.
I love my child
Please help my child to grow up
Without the constant fear that I have had
The fear of one man, one button and a bomb
They can kill the world 1,000 times
Once is enough to kill my child
Why can they shatter our dreams?

Ian McLaughlin

Childhood Fragments

Weren't young, young enough for excuse;
Fingers locked reaching dug shale
One broke free, always washed
Bones, and ruined abbeys
Bloody poppies dotted greystone wall
Stripey, stuck to ragwort like welts
Orchids among the tennis - poorly played.
The odd lost lake, peaty rivers' children
Sausages with sand and flies
Bottles wrapped in wet newspaper, buried.

Summer storms; crisps by candlelight.
Why? are candles dripless?. . . now.

Lisè Watson

Alone

It's dark in here,
Inside this soul,
Where flowers used to grow.

It's dark in here,
Inside this head,
That blossomed once with love.

It's dark in here,
Inside this empty vessel,
That once overflowed with happiness.

It's dark in here,
Inside of me,
Because my *'Love'* I cannot see.

Frankie Quinn

Lourdes

The doctor he called you
An accident of birth.

The priest he called you special,
Some fools called you
A cross for my back.

I called you your name.
And treated you the same.
One day I'll take you to Lourdes.

They say you are trapped.
Other's say you are slow.

I say your name
And treat you the same.

One day I'll take you to Lourdes.

Frances Doyle

First Five Days

The cows are small as ants.
The fields rush past.
I'm cringing in my window seat
Just waiting for the blast.
We land.
No zig-zag through the sniper fire
Where are the troops?
I'm reluctant to enquire.

It's dark outside
And every bush conceals a bomb.
At last! A policeman with a gun
(I must ring home and tell my mum!)
People speak and grin at us
But we just cannot understand.
The first victim of the war
Was English, in this hateful land.

We look at, speak to, no-one
And everybody looks at us
We think, Paranoia?
We're not brave enough to take the bus.
I dare not speak - my dulcet tones
Place me right at England's heart,
Beaten up just five days in
Would not be an auspicious start.

Nine years on from those five days
I walk my daughter up the lane,
'Daddy, what you doin?' she asks
In broad Coleraine.

Peter Hough

The Cost of Being Loyal

My first thought was to be dressed in white, and
Stay like this for the rest of my life.
White robes, pure and clean,
Christening robes, they must be seen.

That's lucky they'd say.
Pouring cold water with delight,
Flowing cold water, I felt numb with fright.
Then cover up, and no light.

I was stupid at three,
Told to keep myself clean.
Turned seven dressed again in white,
Now will I be brainwashed for the rest of my life.
Men are dirty, and sex is bad.
Well aren't you a very lucky
Wee girl, to have a mum and a dad?

At ten I felt sad, the cost of being loyal,
Drove me almost mad.

Turned eighteen, married in white.
Boy I'd got the shock of my life.
My soul drained stained, with fright.
Looking back, sometimes I feel sore and very sad.

Mary Quigley

Kangaroo Court

Before the taped evidence
Is recorded
An admission of guilt
Is sought
Like a constitutional
Court questions are asked
As they probe for the truth

But in this court
Impatience is a reality
And if answers arrive
Not confirming the beliefs
Or assumptions of the interrogators
Brutality is the norm

Blow follows blow
As the hapless victim is meted
Fists and boots, fag ends
And gun butts
In due course
Resistance is eroded
(Even the innocent
Admit to betrayal)

A guilt confirmed
By a confession
Recorded on a cassette

Death usually follows

Liam O'Comáin

The Singing Soldier

The machine gun stood applauding, as the chorus fled his lips,
And paused when he lay sprawling, in the mire of his ditch.
He had sung his words of wisdom, sincerely from his heart,
And for reconciliation, from this world he did depart.
He was just one more statistic, in their catalogue of death,
But his family, friends and comrades, they never shall forget.
    An infant in his cradle, the precious gift of life,
        His parents proud and grateful, such joy should grace their lives.
    A boy played in the school yard, a conker in his hand,
        The pranks, the cane, the bullying, of a generation damned.
    A youth kissed Nancy Glover, neath a weeping willow tree,
        Then carved their names together, for everyone to see.
    A man put on his uniform, then waved his home goodbye,
        And marched off to those bloody fields, where Europe's son's
                      would die.

A voice of peace is silenced, by the justice of a gun,
While generals drunk on cognac, prolong a war benumbed.

Paul Hutton

Promenade

Bewildered by the contours
Of an unforgiving landscape
Crudely defined on a stranger's map,
They stumble for cover
Through townlands they misname
Or slouch exhausted
Along dissident streets
To garrison the past
And watch through gun-sights
While time sweeps by.

Paul Laughlin

The Nightmare

The bed began to move
Clockwise,
In an uneven plane.
The room revolved,
Anti-clockwise
And I descended
A multi-coloured helix.
Accelerating madly,
The surrounding walls
Blurred.
My stomach heaved
Towards my mouth.
Terrified,
I whirled off
The last thread
Of the horror screw.
Cartwheeling
In a void
I fell....... fell......... fell
Through the bottom
Of the well.
I yelled and yelled
But couldn't shout.
At last, my terror
Rang out!

R G Harkness

The Mirage Fades as the Cold Appears

A vision of beauty discomforts my thoughts,
I'd like to think I took the easy way out,
I always dreamed of moments like this,
Always knew how to control reality,
Mixed up ideas of far away places,
Forgotten dreams and realisations,
When will I ever get off this steam train?
Maybe it will slow down if I stop dreaming,
Maybe it will stop, if I start believing.

Terence S McGivern

Realisations

In between hours, broken down messages
Disinformation is our only indication,
That we are not wholly real,
But merely a substitution,
With nothing to play for,
Except an admission,
From the ruling institution
That we are a people,
Of a forgotten population.

Seamus Sarsfield

Spider Spell

The spider now upon the wall
Is long of legs and body small,
Yet, so unlike the fly it kills
It takes its time and stays quite still,
No need has it of nervous flight
Never banging against the light
It casts its spell in a corner
Stops and waits like a sad mourner
Until chance causes it to pounce,
All legs embracing a fly lunch.

Liam Black

Dawn's Early Light

Where shadow lurks in darkened door
And silence reigns supreme
Steals softly in the healing light
To stifle night's extreme.

The darkness backs away and shrinks
Before the awesome might
Of days awakening child that is
Dawn's early light.

Norman Newell